ACTION SCIENCE

THE SCIENCE OF A ROCK CONCERT

SOUND IN ACTION

by Kathy Allen

Consultant:
Paul Ohmann, PhD
Associate Professor of Physics
University of St. Thomas, St. Paul, Minnesota

CAPSTONE PRESS
a capstone imprint

Fact Finders is published by Capstone Press,
151 Good Counsel Drive, P.O. Box 669, Mankato, Minnesota 56002.
www.capstonepress.com

092009
005620LKS10

Books published by Capstone Press are manufactured with paper
containing at least 10 percent post-consumer waste.

Library of Congress Cataloging-in-Publication Data
Allen, Kathy.
    The science of a rock concert : sound in action / by Kathy Allen.
    p. cm. — (Fact finders. Action science)
    Includes bibliographical references and index.
    Summary:"Describes the science behind rock concerts, including sound waves, instruments, sound systems, and
acoustics"— Provided by publisher.
    ISBN 978-1-4296-3956-9 (library binding)
    ISBN 978-1-4296-4857-8 (paperback)
    1. Music — Acoustics and physics — Juvenile literature. 2. Rock concerts — Juvenile literature. I. Title.
II. Series.
ML3805.A45 2010
781.66'143 — dc22   2009033242

Editorial Credits
Lori Shores, editor; Lori Bye, designer; Jo Miller, media researcher; Eric Manske, production specialist

Photo Credits:
Alamy/ABN Stock Images, 11
Getty Images Inc./Bryan Bedder, 23; Dave Etheridge-Barnes, 7; Ethan Miller, 21 (right); FilmMagic/Joey Foley, 10 (left); Jason
    Kempin, 8; Matt Cardy, 17; Michael Buckner, 10 (right); Noel Vasquez, 27; Redferns/Mick Hutson, 9; Redferns/Steve Thorne,
    12; Rick Diamond, 14; Scott Gries, 20; Simone Joyner, 15; WireImage/Eddie Malluk, 19; WireImage/Jason Kempin, 26;
    WireImage/Jon Furniss, 21 (left)
Shutterstock/Amra Pasic, 5; Christoph Weihs, 18; Darko Novakovic, cover; Darren Baker, 16 (bottom right); Lebedinski Vladislav,
    16; Losevsky Pavel, 24–25; M_ART, 29 (bottom); morchella, 13; Noel Powell, Schaumburg, 2–3 (design element); Oguz Aral,
    29 (top); Whaldener Endo, 28

Essential content terms are **bold** and are defined at the bottom of the page where they first appear.

TABLE OF CONTENTS

WIRED FOR SOUND

A crowd streams into a downtown arena. Inside, the stage is wired for sound. At the center of the stage stands the most important member of the band's crew. The chief sound technician says, "check one, check two" into a microphone. The sound carries 300 feet (91 meters) away. As the crowd enters, they hear the sound tech loud and clear.

The sound tech is like a magician who works with the science of sound. From beginning to end, the experience of a rock concert is about sound waves. These waves pulse all around you, even though you can't see them.

Sound waves come from **vibrations**. Put your hand on your throat and say the sound tech's line, check one, check two. Feel that vibration? That's the movement of your vocal cords. When your vocal cords move, they push the air around them outward. Waves of air molecules move until they flow into the ear. The brain understands these movements as sound.

———•———

vibration — a fast, back and forth movement

Thanks to the science of sound, every member of the audience can hear the music coming from the stage.

The audience members have no idea they're about to witness the science of sound in action. They came to the concert for the music. But there would be no music without sound waves.

Each instrument works with the sound system to play tunes familiar to the audience. The sound waves traveling from the stage to the audience are just as thrilling as the rock songs. But the audience members aren't thinking about sound waves. They have their tickets, and they're ready to rock.

SEE FOR YOURSELF

Put a plastic ruler flat on a table. Slide about half of the ruler over the edge of the table. Pluck the end of the ruler with your fingers, as you would pluck a guitar string. That's a sound you can hear and a vibration you can see.

sound waves

Sound waves are like ripples in water, but they're not flat.
They're more like circles that grow outward in a series of waves.

CHAPTER 1

THE SETUP

The sound tech works with the sound waves coming from the instruments. To pump the music out over the whole crowd, the technician uses a sound system. The sound system changes the small sound of a plucked guitar string into a full, booming sound. Without the sound system equipment, audience members sitting far from the stage would be left straining to hear.

A set of powerful speakers is an important part of a sound system at a rock concert.

speaker

feedback

Feedback sounds like a loud, screeching whistle or howl.

Using Feedback

Feedback is the sound you hear when a microphone is too close to a speaker. The sound waves coming from the speaker are "fed back" into the microphone. Then they're sent through the speaker and back to the microphone over and over in a loop. In the 1960s, the Beatles were the first band to use feedback in a song. Today, many musicians use feedback as part of their sound.

MICROPHONES

Fans cheer as the first notes of the night reach their ears. The sound they hear has been on an amazing journey. First microphones pick up sound waves from each instrument. To help you hear, your ear has a tiny **diaphragm** that vibrates when hit by sound waves. At a rock concert, the microphones work the same way. In the microphone, the vibration moves a magnet and wire coil, which turns the sound waves into electrical signals.

————•————

diaphragm — a membrane that vibrates to receive or produce sound

SOUND MIXERS AND AMPLIFIERS

The audience is caught up in the sights and sounds of the concert. But the crowd pays little attention to some nearby equipment. This equipment plays a big part in keeping the show going. The sound tech uses a sound mixer to combine the electrical signals coming from the microphones. The signals are then sent to an **amplifier**. The amplifier boosts them into more powerful signals that will make a louder sound.

━━━●━━━

amplifier — a device used to make sounds louder or stronger

The sound tech progams the sound mixer before the concert. The sounds are adjusted automatically during the concert based on the levels the sound tech sets before the show.

sound mixer

LOUDSPEAKERS

The lead guitarist launches into a rockin' guitar solo. The music booms out of speakers placed all around the stage. The speakers do more than crank out loud music. They turn the electrical signals from the amplifier back into sound waves. Why? Because you can't hear an electrical signal. It's the physical energy of sound waves that you can hear.

diaphragm

Like your ears and the microphones, speakers have one or more diaphragms. If you look closely at a speaker, you can see these cone-shaped structures inside.

Electrical signals vibrate the speaker to produce sound waves. The waves are like the ones created when the guitarist first plucked a string. But now, the sound waves have more energy, which gives them more **intensity** and more volume. For example, a guitar string plucked softly creates a less intense sound with less energy. The sound made by a more forceful pluck of the string is louder and more intense. The intensity of a sound is measured in decibels (dBs). A loud concert can measure about 115 to 120 dBs. Compare that to a whisper, which is only 20 dBs!

intensity — the amount of energy in a sound wave that passes through a certain area every second

SEE FOR YOURSELF

Turn on your radio and put your hand on the speaker. You should be able to feel it vibrating. Now hold a blown-up balloon next to the speaker. See what happens when you turn the volume up!

13

CHAPTER 2

SHOWTIME

The screaming fans can't drown out the band's instruments. The chords of their biggest hit are strummed on the guitar. The lead singer hits all the right notes. Every note the band plays is made of evenly spaced sound waves, which are measured by **frequency**. When the waves are close together, the sound has a higher frequency. Sounds with a higher frequency have a higher **pitch**. When sound waves are farther apart, the frequency and pitch are lower.

frequency — the number of sound waves that pass a location in a certain amount of time
pitch — how high or low a sound is

Drum sets can be tuned to raise or lower the pitch of the drums.

Each instrument delivers sound waves in a different way. You might think of pitch as a high note or a low note. But the same note played on a piano sounds different on a saxophone. That's the quality of the note, or its **timbre**. Sound quality varies from instrument to instrument.

timbre — the quality of a sound that makes one voice or instrument different from another

THE INSTRUMENTS

The guitarist's fingers are a blur of movement as they move across the strings. All the plucking and strumming changes the pitch of the sound waves coming from the instrument. Pressing the strings in different areas of the guitar's neck shortens the length of the strings. The shorter the string is when plucked, the faster the string vibrates, creating a higher pitch.

neck

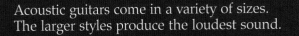
Acoustic guitars come in a variety of sizes. The larger styles produce the loudest sound.

The face of an acoustic guitar is called the soundboard. The soundboard is one part of the guitar's hollow body. The body vibrates when the strings do. Sound waves **resonate**, or bounce around, inside the guitar before they're released through the hole on the soundboard. This movement is what makes the full, rich sound.

resonate — to continue a sound by reflecting it off a surface or by vibrating a nearby object at the same time

17

An electric guitar also has strings, but it doesn't have a hollow body to amplify sound. In fact, if you strum an electric guitar that's not plugged in, you can barely hear it. An electric guitar picks up the vibration of the strings with a magnet called a pickup. When the guitar is plugged in, the pickup turns the sound waves into electrical signals. From there, the signals are sent through the sound mixer and amplifier. Finally the signals make it to the speakers where they're turned back into sound waves.

Electric bass guitars have four strings instead of six. The strings produce lower pitches than the lead guitar.

pickup

SEE FOR YOURSELF

Take the ruler you used on page 6. By putting more of the ruler on the table, you shorten the part of the ruler you pluck. Like pressing strings on a guitar's neck, this action will change the sound you create by plucking. Pluck it at several different lengths. Can you hear the difference?

The saxophonist presses keys on the instrument's body to change the pitch of the sound waves as he plays.

Every instrument on stage adds to the music by making a physical vibration. At the end of the guitar solo, the saxophone blares. As the saxophonist plays, a wooden reed vibrates on the instrument's mouthpiece. The sound made by the vibrations resonates in the body before ringing out through the large opening. The keyboardist jumps in and strikes keys on the electric piano. Each key moves a hammer to hit a string and start a vibration. The drummer joins by pounding on the top of the drums. The sound resonates inside the drum.

All the sound waves blend together to make the familiar melody that every member of the band plays. From strings, reeds, and drums to eardrums, vibrations travel through the air. The audience can feel the energy coming from the stage.

The drummer also plays cymbals attached to his drum set. Larger and heavier cymbals produce louder sound.

cymbal

CHAPTER 3

ENCORE!

The audience screams for more as the band leaves the stage. After a few minutes, the band returns to play an old favorite for their loyal fans. Thanks to the planning that went into the arena, the encore sounds just as sweet as the opening number.

Engineers pay special attention to **acoustics** when they build concert halls. The best halls block outside noise. But they also work with the sound waves inside to create a good environment for the best sound. Sound waves don't disappear when they hit walls, people, or chairs. They are either absorbed or reflected. The engineers know that the materials inside the hall determine how much sound gets absorbed or reflected.

———◆———

acoustics — the qualities in an enclosed space that make it easy or hard for a person in it to hear

The acoustics of the Beacon Theatre in New York has made it a favorite among muscians and concertgoers.

SEE FOR YOURSELF

Next time you're in the shower, belt out your favorite song. Notice how the tiles and glass make the sound echo? Compare that to singing in a carpeted room. The carpet absorbs sound waves, while the tiles reflect them.

Sound Waves in Action

Wood walls and ceiling reflect sound.

Stage floor reflects sound waves out into concert hall.

When sound waves hit a hard surface, such as steel or concrete, some of them are bounced back. This action creates an echo. Imagine standing in your school's gym. You yell, "helloooo!" and the walls yell it right back to you. This reflected sound is fun in the gym. But in a concert hall, reflected sound can be muddled or confusing.

Bowl shape keeps the sound waves moving around the hall.

Cushions on seats help to absorb sound waves.

Some materials absorb sound waves. Rubber and fiberglass absorb some of the sound waves. Even chair cushions and carpet reduce the reflection of sound in the room. These materials don't absorb all the sound. Enough sound waves are reflected by hard surfaces to create a big sound that seems to surround the audience.

Outdoor Concerts

At an outdoor concert, there are few surfaces to reflect sound. Most sound waves are absorbed by trees or grass, or they die in the air. But sound waves can't travel long distances. Speakers placed around the park carry the music to people 1,000 feet (305 meters) away. It takes a big sound system for everyone to hear the music.

A lot of equipment is needed to put on a great concert. The sound equipment works hard behind the scenes to bring the science of sound to life.

As the crowd leaves the arena, new sounds reach their ears. Thousands of shuffling feet and car horns replace the music of the band. The concert is over, but sounds are everywhere. Fans talk about the spectacular sounds of the rock concert. They marvel at the best songs of the night. The band was as rockin' as ever. And even though the fans aren't talking about it, the science of sound was the star of the night.

ROCKIN' FACTS

• The first rock concert for the hearing impaired was held in Toronto, Canada, in 2009. The audience members sat in chairs designed to amplify the sounds and vibrate along with the music. They felt the music through their skin. The skin is a membrane, just like the eardrum.

• Stonehenge, the giant circle of standing stones in England, is a mystery. But some scientists believe it was once a huge concert hall. They think music would have resonated within the circle to produce an intense, dramatic sound.

Stonehenge

• No one knows exactly how loud a sound has to be to cause hearing damage. Scientists believe damage is caused by sounds between 120 and 140 decibels. But listening to sounds above 90 decibels for a long time can also cause damage to hearing.

OTHER SCIENCES IN ACTION

The Human Ear — The eardrum vibrates at the same frequency of the sound you hear. Tiny hairlike structures in the inner ear are each sensitive to specific frequencies.

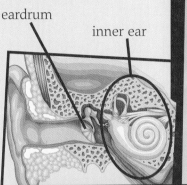

eardrum

inner ear

cross section of human ear

Heat — When an object heats up, tiny parts called atoms move faster. They bounce off other atoms, making them hotter too. Light energy can change into heat. An indoor concert uses electrical energy to shine spotlights on the band, making even the coolest musicians sweat.

Light — Sound and heat aren't the only kind of energy at a rock concert. Light is a form of energy that makes everything around you visible. But just seeing the band isn't enough at some shows. Some bands use amazing light shows to add energy to the event.

Glossary

acoustics (uh-KOO-stiks) — the qualities in an enclosed space that make it easy or hard for a person in it to hear

amplifier (AM-pluh-fye-uhr) — a device used to make sounds louder or stronger

diaphragm (DYE-uh-fram) — a thin, flexible membrane that vibrates to receive or produce sound waves

frequency (FREE-kwuhn-see) — the number of sound waves that pass a location in a certain amount of time

intensity (in-TEN-suh-tee) — the amount of energy in a sound wave that passes through a certain area every second

molecule (MOL-uh-kyool) — the smallest part of an element that can exist and still keep the characteristics of the element

pitch (PICH) — the highness or lowness of a sound

resonate (REZ-uh-nayt) — to continue a sound by reflecting it off a surface or by vibrating a nearby object at the same time

timbre (TAM-burr) — the quality of a sound that makes one voice or instrument different from another

vibration (vye-BRAY-shun) — a fast, back and forth movement of an object or wave

Read More

Hewitt, Sally. *Sound.* Starting Science. New York: Franklin Watts, 2009.

Oxlade, Chris. *Experiments with Sound: Explaining Sound.* Do It Yourself. Chicago: Heinemann, 2009.

Parker, Steve. *Earsplitters!: The World's Loudest Noises.* Extreme! Mankato, Minn.: Capstone Press, 2009.

Sohn, Emily. *Adventures in Sound with Max Axiom, Super Scientist.* Graphic Science. Mankato, Minn.: Capstone Press, 2007.

Internet Sites

FactHound offers a safe, fun way to find Internet sites related to this book. All of the sites on FactHound have been researched by our staff.

Here's all you do:

Visit *www.facthound.com*

FactHound will fetch the best sites for you!

Index